Born in 1979

By

Kerry Butters.

Born in 1979

Millennium:	**2nd millennium**
Centuries:	19th century – **20th century** – 21st century
Decades:	1940s 1950s 1960s – **1970s** – 1980s 1990s 2000s
Years:	1976 1977 1978 – **1979** – 1980 1981 1982

1979 (MCMLXXIX) was a common year starting on Monday (dominical letter G) of the Gregorian calendar, the 1979th year of the Common Era (CE) and *Anno Domini* (AD) designations, the 979th year of the 2nd millennium, the 79th year of the 20th century, and the 10th and last year of the 1970s decade.

Contents

- 1 Events
- 2 Births
- 3 Deaths
- 4 Nobel Prizes
- 5 In the News

Events

January

- January 1
  - United Nations Secretary-General Kurt Waldheim heralds the start of the *International Year of the Child*. Many musicians donate to the *Music for UNICEF Concert* fund including ABBA, who wrote the song "Chiquitita" to commemorate the event.
  - The United States and the People's Republic of China establish full diplomatic relations.
  - The Canton of Jura comes into existence as the 26th canton of Switzerland, being formed from the predominantly French-speaking Catholic part of the Canton of Bern.
  - Following a deal agreed during 1978, French carmaker Peugeot completes a takeover of American manufacturer Chrysler's European operations, which are based in Britain's former Rootes Group factories as well as the former Simca factories in France.
- January 4 – The State of Ohio agrees to pay $675,000 to families of the dead and injured in the Kent State shootings.
- January 5 – Queen releases "Don't Stop Me Now". It becomes one of their most popular singles.
- January 7 – Vietnam and Vietnam-backed Cambodian insurgents announce the fall of Phnom Penh, Cambodia, and the collapse of the Pol Pot regime. Pol Pot and the Khmer Rouge retreat west to an area along the Thai border.

- January 8 – Whiddy Island Disaster: The French tanker *Betelgeuse* explodes at the Gulf Oil terminal at Bantry, Ireland; 50 are killed.
- January 9 – The *Music for UNICEF Concert* is held at the United Nations General Assembly to raise money for UNICEF and promote the Year of the Child. It is broadcast the following day in the United States and around the world. Hosted by the Bee Gees, other performers include Donna Summer, ABBA, Rod Stewart and Earth, Wind & Fire. A soundtrack album is later released.
- January 16 – Shah Mohammad Reza Pahlavi flees Iran with his family, relocating to Egypt after a year of turmoil.
- January 19 – Former U.S. Attorney General John N. Mitchell is released on parole after 19 months at a federal prison in Alabama.
- January 25 – Pope John Paul II arrives in Mexico City for his first visit to Mexico, mainly for 1979's Latin American Episcopal Conference (CELAM) or Conference of Puebla.
- January 26 – *The Dukes of Hazzard* debuts on CBS.
- January 29 – Brenda Ann Spencer opens fire at a school in San Diego, killing 2 faculty members and wounding 8 students and a police officer. Her justification for the action, "I don't like Mondays", inspires the Boomtown Rats to make a song of the same name.

February

- February 1 – Ayatollah Ruhollah Khomeini returns to Tehran, Iran after nearly 15 years of exile.
- February 2
  - Former Sex Pistols bassist Sid Vicious is found dead, aged 21, of a heroin overdose in New York City, the day after being released from a 55-day sentence at Rikers Island prison on bail.
- February 3 – Ayatollah Khomeini creates the Council of the Islamic Revolution.
- February 7
  - Iranian Revolution: Supporters of Ayatollah Khomeini take over the Iranian law enforcement, courts and government

administration; the final session of the Iranian National Consultative Assembly is held.

- o Pluto moves inside Neptune's orbit for the first time since either was known to science.
- o Nazi criminal Josef Mengele suffers a stroke and drowns while swimming in Bertioga, Brazil. His remains are found in 1985.
- February 10–11 – Iranian Revolution: The Iranian army withdraws to its barracks leaving power in the hands of Ayatollah Khomeini, ending the Pahlavi dynasty.
- February 12 – Prime Minister Hissène Habré starts the Battle of N'Djamena in an attempt to overthrow Chad's President Félix Malloum.
- February 13 – The intense February 13, 1979 windstorm strikes western Washington and sinks a 1/2-mile-long section of the Hood Canal Bridge.
- February 14
  - o In Kabul, Muslim extremists kidnap the American ambassador to Afghanistan, Adolph Dubs, who is later killed during a gunfight between his kidnappers and police.
  - o Following her 1972 sex reassignment surgery, musician Wendy Carlos legally changes her name from Walter. She reveals this information in an interview in the May 1979 issue of *Playboy* magazine.
- February 15 – A suspected gas explosion in a Warsaw bank kills 49.
- February 17 – The People's Republic of China invades northern Vietnam, launching the Sino-Vietnamese War.
- February 18 – The Sahara Desert experiences snow for 30 minutes.
- February 22 – Saint Lucia becomes independent of the United Kingdom.
- February 24 – Ethiopia recognizes the Sahrawi Arab Democratic Republic (SADR).
- February 26 – A total solar eclipse, the last visible from the continental United States until 2017, arcs over northern coterminous USA and southeastern Canada ending in Greenland.

A partial solar eclipse is visible over almost all of North America and Central America including the eastern half of AK and the western half of UK.

- February 27 – The annual Mardi Gras celebration in New Orleans is cancelled due to a strike called by the New Orleans Police Department.

March

- March 1
  - Scottish devolution referendum: Scotland votes in favour for a Scottish Assembly, which is not implemented due to failing a condition that at least 40% of the electorate must support the proposal; in a Welsh devolution referendum, Wales votes against devolution.
  - Philips publicly demonstrate a prototype of an optical digital audio disc at a press conference in Eindhoven, Netherlands.
- March 4 – The U.S. *Voyager 1* spaceprobe photos reveal Jupiter's rings.
- March 5 – *Voyager 1* makes its closest approach to Jupiter at 172,000 miles.
- March 7 – The largest Magnetar (Soft gamma repeater) event is recorded.
- March 8 – Philips demonstrates the compact disc publicly for the first time.
- March 13 – Maurice Bishop leads a successful coup in Grenada. His government will be crushed by American intervention in 1983.
- March 14 – In China, a Hawker Siddeley Trident crashes into a factory near Beijing, killing at least 200.
- March 16 – End of major hostilities in the Sino-Vietnamese War.
- March 17 – The Penmanshiel Tunnel in the U.K. collapses, killing 2 workers.
- March 18 – Ten miners die in a methane gas explosion at Golborne Colliery near Wigan, Greater Manchester, England.

- March 25 – The first fully functional Space Shuttle orbiter, *Columbia*, is delivered to the Kennedy Space Center, to be prepared for its first launch.
- March 26
    - In a ceremony at the White House, President Anwar Sadat of Egypt and Prime Minister Menachem Begin of Israel sign an Egypt–Israel Peace Treaty.
    - Michigan State University, led by Earvin "Magic" Johnson, defeats Larry Bird-led Indiana State 75-64 in the NCAA tournmaent championship game at Salt Lake City.
- March 28
    - In Britain, James Callaghan's minority Labour government loses a motion of confidence by 1 vote, forcing a general election which is to be held on 3 May.
    - America's most serious nuclear power plant accident occurs, at Three Mile Island, Pennsylvania.
- March 29 – Sultan Yahya Petra of Kelantan, the 6th Yang di-Pertuan Agong (Head of State) of Malaysia, dies in office. He is replaced by Sultan Ahmad Shah of Pahang.
- March 30 – Airey Neave, World War II veteran and Conservative Northern Ireland spokesman, is killed by an Irish National Liberation Army bomb in the British House of Commons car park.
- March 31
    - The last British soldier (belonging to the Royal Navy) leaves the Maltese Islands, after 179 years of presence. Malta declares its Freedom Day (Jum il-Helsien).
    - Gali Atari and Milk and Honey win the Eurovision Song Contest 1979 for Israel, with the song "Hallelujah".

April

- April 1
    - Iran's government becomes an Islamic Republic by a 98% vote, overthrowing the Shah officially.

- The Pinwheel Network changes its name to Nickelodeon and begins airing on various Warner Cable systems beginning in Buffalo, New York, expanding its audience reach.
- April 1 – April 18 – Police lock Andreas Mihavecz in a holding cell in Bregenz, Austria and forget about him, leaving him there without food or drink.
- April 2 – Sverdlovsk anthrax leak: A Soviet biowarfare laboratory at Sverdlovsk accidentally releases airborne anthrax spores, killing 66 plus an unknown amount of livestock. It is a violation of the Biological Weapons Convention of 1972.
- April 6 – Student protests break out in Nepal.
- April 7 – In Japan, Yoshiyuki Tomino directed *Mobile Suit Gundam*, the first series of the metaseries of the same name.
- April 10
  - A tornado hits Wichita Falls, Texas, killing 42 people (the most notable of 26 tornadoes that day).
  - Cambodia recognizes the Sahrawi Arab Democratic Republic (SADR).
- April 11 – Tanzanian troops take Kampala, the capital of Uganda; Idi Amin flees.
- April 13 – The La Soufrière volcano erupts in St. Vincent and the Grenadines.
- April 15 – 1979 Montenegro earthquake: A major earthquake (7.0 on the Richter scale) strikes Montenegro (then part of Yugoslavia) and parts of Albania, causing extensive damage to coastal areas and taking 136 lives; the old town of Budva is devastated.
- April 17 – Schoolchildren in the Central African Republic are arrested (and around 100 killed) for protesting against compulsory school uniforms. An African judicial commission later determines that Emperor Jean-Bédel Bokassa "almost certainly" took part in the massacre.
- April 20 – President Jimmy Carter is attacked by a swamp rabbit while fishing in his hometown of Plains, Georgia, USA.
- April 22 – The Albert Einstein Memorial is unveiled at The National Academy of Sciences in Washington, D.C.

- April 23 – Fighting breaks out in London between the Anti-Nazi League and the Metropolitan Police's Special Patrol Group; protester Blair Peach receives fatal injuries during the incident, now officially attributed to the SPG.

May

May 4: Margaret Thatcher becomes the country's first female prime minister

- May 1 – Greenland is granted limited autonomy from Denmark, with its own Parliament sitting in Nuuk.
- May 4 – Counting in the previous day's British general election shows that the Conservatives have won and Margaret Thatcher becomes the country's first female prime minister, ending the rule of James Callaghan's Labour government.
- May 8 – The Woolworth's store in Manchester city centre in England is seriously damaged by fire; 10 shoppers die.
- May 9
    - The Salvadoran Civil War begins.
    - A Unabomber bomb injures Northwestern University graduate student John Harris.
    - Laos recognizes the Sahrawi Arab Democratic Republic (SADR).
- May 10 – The Federated States of Micronesia becomes self-governing.
- May 21
    - Dan White receives a light sentence for killing San Francisco Mayor George Moscone and Supervisor Harvey Milk, gay men in the city riot.

- May 23 – Afghanistan recognizes the Sahrawi Arab Democratic Republic (SADR).
- May 25
  - American Airlines Flight 191: In Chicago, a DC-10 crashes during takeoff at O'Hare International Airport, killing all 271 on board and 2 people on the ground in the deadliest aviation accident in U. S. history.
  - John Spenkelink is executed in Florida, in the first use of the electric chair in America after the reintroduction of the death penalty in 1976.
  - Etan Patz, 6 years old, is kidnapped in New York. He is often referred to as the "Boy on the Milk Carton" and the investigation later sprouts into one of the most prolific child abduction cases of all time. This is a cold case until 2010 when it is re-opened.
- May 27 – Indianapolis 500: Rick Mears wins the race for the first time, and car owner Roger Penske for the second time.

June

- June – McDonald's introduces the Happy Meal.
- June 1
  - The Vizianagaram district is formed in Andhra Pradesh, India.
  - The first black-led government of Rhodesia in 90 years takes power, in succession to Ian Smith and under his power-sharing deal.
  - The Seattle SuperSonics win the NBA Championship against the Washington Bullets.
- June 2
  - Pope John Paul II arrives in his native Poland on his first official, nine-day stay, becoming the first Pope to visit a Communist country. This visit, known as nine days that changed the world, brings about the solidarity of the Polish people against Communism, ultimately leading to the rise of the Solidarity movement.

- Los Angeles' city council passes the city's first homosexual rights bill signed without fanfare by mayor Thomas Bradley.
- June 3
  - A blowout at the Ixtoc I oil well in the southern Gulf of Mexico causes at least 600,000 tons (176,400,000 gallons) of oil to be spilled into the waters, the worst oil spill to date. Some estimate the spill to be 428 million gallons, making it the largest unintentional oil spill until it was surpassed by the Deepwater Horizon oil spill in 2010.
  - General elections are held in Italy.
- June 4
  - Joe Clark becomes Canada's 16th and youngest Prime Minister.
  - Flight Lieutenant Jerry Rawlings takes power in Ghana after a military coup in which General Fred Akuffo is overthrown.
- June 7 – The first direct elections to the European Parliament begin, allowing citizens from across all then-9 European Community member states to elect 410 MEPs. It is also the first international election in history.
- June 12 – Bryan Allen flies the man-powered Gossamer Albatross across the English Channel.
- June 18 – Jimmy Carter and Leonid Brezhnev sign the SALT II agreement in Vienna.
- June 20 – A Nicaraguan National Guard soldier kills ABC TV news correspondent Bill Stewart and his interpreter Juan Espinosa. Other members of the news crew capture the killing on tape.
- June 23 – Sydney: New South Wales Premier Neville Wran officially opens the Eastern Suburbs Railway. It operates as a shuttle between Central & Bondi Junction until full integration with the Illawarra Line in 1980.
- June 24 – Bologna: The Permanent Peoples' Tribunal, an international opinion tribunal, is founded at the initiative of Senator Lelio Basso.
- June 25 – Belgium: NATO Supreme Allied Commander Alexander Haig escapes an assassination attempt by the Baader-Meinhof terrorist organization.

July

- July 1
  - Sweden outlaws corporal punishment in the home.
  - The Sony Walkman goes on sale for the first time in Japan.
- July 3 – U.S. President Jimmy Carter signs the first directive for secret aid to the opponents of the pro-Soviet regime in Kabul.
- July 4 – Cape Verde recognizes the Sahrawi Arab Democratic Republic.
- July 5 – Queen Elizabeth II attends the millennium celebrations of the Isle of Man's Parliament, Tynwald.
- July 8 – Los Angeles passes its gay and lesbian civil rights bill.
- July 9 – A car bomb destroys a Renault owned by Nazi hunters Serge and Beate Klarsfeld at their home in France. A note purportedly from ODESSA claims responsibility.
- July 11 – NASA's first orbiting space station *Skylab* begins its return to Earth, after being in orbit for 6 years and 2 months.
- July 12
  - The Gilbert Islands become fully independent of the United Kingdom as Kiribati.
  - A *Disco Demolition Night* publicity stunt goes awry at Comiskey Park, forcing the Chicago White Sox to forfeit their game against the Detroit Tigers.
  - Carmine Galante, boss of the Bonanno crime family, is assassinated in Brooklyn.
  - A fire at a hotel in Zaragoza, Spain, leaves 72 dead, the worst hotel fire in Europe in decades.
- July 16 – Iraqi President Hasan al-Bakr resigns and Vice President Saddam al-Tikriti replaces him.
- July 17 – Nicaraguan dictator General Anastasio Somoza Debayle resigns and flees to Miami.
- July 21
  - The Sandinista National Liberation Front concludes a successful revolutionary campaign against the U.S.-backed Somoza dictatorship and assumes power in Nicaragua.

- Maria de Lourdes Pintasilgo becomes prime minister of Portugal.
- Maritza Sayalero of Venezuela wins the Miss Universe pageant; the stage collapses after contestants and news photographers rush to her throne.
- The Disco music genre dominates and peaks on the *Billboard* Hot 100 chart, with the first six spots (beginning with Donna Summer's *Bad Girls*), and seven of the chart's top ten songs ending that week.

August

- August 3 – Dictator Francisco Macías Nguema of Equatorial Guinea is overthrown in a bloody coup d'état led by Teodoro Obiang Nguema Mbasogo.
- August 4 – Opening game of the *American Football Bundesliga* played between Frankfurter Löwen and Düsseldorf Panther, first-ever league game of American football in Germany.
- August 5 – The Polisario Front signs a peace treaty with Mauritania. Mauritania withdraws from the Western Sahara territory it had occupied, and cedes it to the SADR.
- August 8 – Two American commercial divers, Richard Walker and Victor Guiel, die of hypothermia after their diving bell becomes stranded at a depth of over 160 metres (520 ft) in the East Shetland Basin. The legal repercussions of the accident will lead to important safety changes in the diving industry.
- August 9
  - A nudist beach is established in Brighton.
  - Raymond Washington, co-founder of the Crips, today one of the largest, most notorious gangs in the United States, is killed in a drive-by shooting in Los Angeles (his killers have not yet been identified).
- August 10 – Michael Jackson releases his breakthrough album *Off the Wall*. It sells 7 million copies in the United States alone, making it a 7x platinum album.

- August 11 – The former Mauritanian province of Tiris al-Gharbiyya in Western Sahara is annexed by Morocco.
- August 14 – A freak storm during the Fastnet Race results in the deaths of 15 sailors.
- August 20 – Grenada recognizes the Sahrawi Arab Democratic Republic (SADR).
- August 24 – Ghana recognizes the Sahrawi Arab Democratic Republic (SADR).
- August 27 – Lord Mountbatten of Burma and 3 others are assassinated by the Provisional Irish Republican Army. He was a British admiral, statesman and an uncle of The Duke of Edinburgh. On the same day, the Warrenpoint ambush occurs, killing 18 British soldiers.
- August 28 – The death toll of the previous day's IRA bombing reaches 5 when Doreen Knatchbull, Baroness Brabourne, 83, dies in a hospital as a result of her injuries.
- August 29 – A national referendum is held in which Somali voters approve a new liberal constitution, promulgated by President Siad Barre to placate the United States.

September

- September 1
  - The U.S. *Pioneer 11* becomes the first spacecraft to visit Saturn, when it passes the planet at a distance of 21,000 km.
  - Dominica, Guyana & St. Lucia recognize the Sahrawi Arab Democratic Republic (SADR).
  - Sri Lanka Army Women's Corps is formed.
- September 4 – Jamaica recognizes the Sahrawi Arab Democratic Republic (SADR).
- September 6 – Nicaragua and Uganda recognize the Sahrawi Arab Democratic Republic (SADR).
- September 7 – The first cable sports channel, ESPN, known as the Entertainment Sports Programming Network, is launched.
- September 8 – Mexico recognizes the Sahrawi Arab Democratic Republic (SADR).

- September 9 – The long-running comic strip *For Better or For Worse* begins its run.
- September 12 – Hurricane Frederic makes landfall at 10:00 p.m. on Alabama's Gulf Coast.
- September 16 – Two families flee from East Germany by balloon.
- September 20 – French paratroopers help David Dacko to overthrow Bokassa in the Central African Republic.
- September 22 – The South Atlantic Flash is observed near the Prince Edward Islands, thought to be a nuclear weapons test conducted by South Africa and Israel.
- September 30 – The Hong Kong MTR begins service with the opening of its Modified Initial System (aka Kwun Tong Line).

October

- October 1 – Nigeria terminates military rule, and the Second Nigerian Republic is established.
- October 1 – October 6 – Pope John Paul II visits the United States.
- October 1 – The MTR, the rapid transit railway system in Hong Kong, opens.
- October 3 – An EF4 Tornado hits Windsor Locks, Connecticut, causing extensive damage to the town.
- October 6 – Federal Reserve System changes from an interest rate target policy to a money supply target policy.
- October 9
  - Peter Brock wins the Bathurst 1000 by a record 6 laps, with a lap record on the last lap.
  - Lesotho recognizes the Sahrawi Arab Democratic Republic (SADR).
- October 12
  - Zambia recognizes the Sahrawi Arab Democratic Republic (SADR).
  - Near Guam, Typhoon Tip reaches a record intensity of 870 millibars, the lowest pressure recorded at sea level. This makes Tip the most powerful tropical cyclone in known world history.

- o Thorbjörn Fälldin returns as Prime Minister of Sweden , replacing Ola Ullsten who becomes Foreign Minister of Sweden .
- October 14 – A major gay rights march in the United States takes place in Washington, D.C., involving tens of thousands of people.
- October 15 – Black Monday events, in which members of a political group sack a newspaper office, unfold in Malta.
- October 16 – A tsunami in Nice, France kills 23 people.
- October 19 – 13 U.S. Marines die in a fire at Camp Fuji, Japan as a result of Typhoon Tip.
- October 20 – The first McDonald's in Singapore opens at Liat Towers in Orchard Road.
- October 26 – Park Chung-hee, the President of South Korea, is assassinated by KCIA director Kim Jae-gyu.
- October 27 – Saint Vincent and the Grenadines gains independence from the United Kingdom.

November

- November 1 – Iran hostage crisis: Iranian Ayatollah Ruhollah Khomeini urges his people to demonstrate on November 4 and to expand attacks on United States and Israeli interests.
- November 2
  - o French police shoot gangster Jacques Mesrine in Paris.
  - o Assata Shakur (née Joanne Chesimard), a former member of the Black Panther Party and Black Liberation Army, escapes from a New York prison to Cuba, where she remains under political asylum.
- November 3 – In Greensboro, North Carolina, 5 members of the Communist Workers Party are shot to death and 7 are wounded by a group of Klansmen and neo-Nazis, during a "Death to the Klan" rally.
- November 4 – Iran hostage crisis begins: 3,000 Iranian radicals, mostly students, invade the U.S. Embassy in Tehran and take 90 hostages (53 of whom are American). They demand that the United States send the former Shah of Iran back to stand trial.

- November 5 – The radio news program *Morning Edition* premieres on National Public Radio in the United States.
- November 6 – At Montevideo, Uruguay, the International Olympic Committee adopts a resolution, whereby Taiwan Olympic and sports teams will participate with the name Chinese Taipei in future Olympic Games and international sports tournaments and championships.
- November 7 – U.S. Senator Ted Kennedy announces that he will challenge President Jimmy Carter for the 1980 Democratic presidential nomination.
- November 9
  - The Carl Bridgewater murder trial ends in England with all 4 men found guilty. James Robinson, 45, and 25-year-old Vincent Hickey are sentenced to life imprisonment with a recommended 25-year minimum for murder. 18-year-old Michael Hickey is also found guilty of murder and sentenced to indefinite detention. Patrick Molloy, 53, is found guilty on a lesser charge of manslaughter and sentenced to 12 years in prison.
  - Nuclear false alarm: the NORAD computers and the Alternate National Military Command Center in Fort Ritchie, Maryland, detect an apparent massive Soviet nuclear strike. After reviewing the raw data from satellites and checking the early-warning radars, the alert is cancelled.
- November 10 – 1979 Mississauga train derailment: A 106-car Canadian Pacific freight train carrying explosive and poisonous chemicals from Windsor, Ontario, Canada derails in Mississauga, Ontario, Canada just west of Toronto, Ontario, Canada, causing a massive explosion and the largest peacetime evacuation in Canadian history and one of the largest in North American history.
- November 12
  - Iran hostage crisis: In response to the hostage situation in Tehran, U.S. President Jimmy Carter orders a halt to all oil imports into the United States from Iran.

- o Süleyman Demirel, of the Justice Party (AP) forms the new government of Turkey (43rd government, a minority government).
- November 14 – Iran hostage crisis: U.S. President Jimmy Carter issues Executive Order 12170, freezing all Iranian assets in the United States and U.S. banks in response to the hostage crisis.
- November 15 – British art historian and former Surveyor of the Queen's Pictures Anthony Blunt's role as the "fourth man" of the 'Cambridge Five' double agents for the Soviet NKVD during World War II is revealed by Prime Minister Margaret Thatcher in the House of Commons of the United Kingdom; she gives further details on November 21.
- November 16 – Bucharest Metro Line One is opened, in Bucharest, Romania (from Timpuri Noi to Semanatoarea stations, 8.63 km).
- November 17 – Iran hostage crisis: Iranian leader Ruhollah Khomeini orders the release of 13 female and African American hostages being held at the U.S. Embassy in Tehran.
- November 20 – Grand Mosque seizure: A group of 200 Juhayman al-Otaybi militants occupy Mecca's Masjid al-Haram, the holiest place in Islam. They are driven out by French commandos (allowed into the city under these special circumstances despite their being non-Muslims) after bloody fighting that leaves 250 people dead and 600 wounded.
- November 21 – After false radio reports from the Ayatollah Khomeini that the Americans had occupied the Grand Mosque in Mecca, the United States Embassy in Islamabad, Pakistan is attacked by a mob and set afire, killing 4, and disturbing Pakistan–United States relations.
- November 23 – In Dublin, Ireland, Provisional Irish Republican Army member Thomas McMahon is sentenced to life in prison for the assassination of Lord Mountbatten of Burma.
- November 25 – Last cargo of phosphate shipped from Banaba Island.
- November 28 – Air New Zealand Flight 901: an Air New Zealand DC-10 crashes into Mount Erebus in Antarctica on a sightseeing trip, killing all 257 people on board.

December

- December 3
  - Eleven fans are killed during a crowd crush for unreserved seats before The Who rock concert at the Riverfront Coliseum in Cincinnati.
  - The United States dollar exchange rate with the Deutsche Mark falls to 1.7079 DM, the all-time low so far; this record is not broken until November 5, 1987.
- December 4 – The Hastie fire in Kingston upon Hull, England, leads to the deaths of 3 boys and begins the hunt for Bruce George Peter Lee, the UK's most prolific killer.
- December 5 – Jack Lynch resigns as Taoiseach of the Republic of Ireland; he is succeeded by Charles Haughey.
- December 6 – The world premiere of *Star Trek: The Motion Picture* is held at the Smithsonian Institution in Washington, D.C.
- December 9 – The eradication of the smallpox virus is certified, making smallpox the first of only two human diseases that have been driven to extinction.
- December 12
  - The 8.2 Mw Tumaco earthquake shakes Colombia and Ecuador with a maximum Mercalli intensity of IX (*Violent*), killing 300–600, and generating a large tsunami.
  - Coup d'état of December Twelfth: South Korean Army Major General Chun Doo-hwan orders the arrest of Army Chief of Staff General Jeong Seung-hwa without authorization from President Choi Kyu-hah, alleging involvement in the assassination of ex-President Park Chung-hee.
  - The unrecognised state of Zimbabwe-Rhodesia returns to British control and resumes using the name Southern Rhodesia.
- December 15 – The directorial debut of Hayao Miyazaki, *The Castle of Cagliostro* based on the manga series *Lupin III* is released in Japan.
- December 21 – A ceasefire for Rhodesia is signed at London.

- December 23 – The highest aerial tramway in Europe, the Klein Matterhorn, opens.
- December 24
  - The Soviet Union invades Afghanistan, and Babrak Karmal replaces overthrown and executed President Hafizullah Amin, which begins the war.
  - The first European Ariane rocket is launched.
- December 26 – In Rhodesia, 96 Patriotic Front guerrillas enter the capital Salisbury to monitor a ceasefire that begins December 28.

Date unknown

- The One-child policy is introduced in China - it has contributed to Missing women of China. It is later loosened in 2013.
- VisiCalc becomes the first commercial spreadsheet program.
- The first usenet experiments are conducted by Tom Truscott and Jim Ellis of Duke University.
- Worldwide per capita oil production reaches a historic peak.
- Chrysler receives government loan guarantees upon the request of CEO Lee Iacocca.
- The remains of Tsar Nicholas II and some of the Romanovs are discovered and exhumed near Sverdlovsk (now Yekaterinburg).

Births

January

Aaliyah

Rosamund Pike

- January 1
  - Brody Dalle, Australian singer
  - Gisela, Spanish pop singer and a Spanish dub actress
  - Koichi Domoto, Japanese entertainer (KinKi Kids)
- January 2
  - Morena Baccarin, Italo-Brazilian actress
  - Erica Hubbard, American actress
- January 3
  - Francesco Bellissimo, Italian Chef
  - Koit Toome, Estonian singer and musical actor
  - Rie Tanaka, Japanese voice actress

- January 6
  - Christina Chanée, Danish-Thai pop singer
  - Bernice Liu, Hong Kong actress
- January 7
  - Bipasha Basu, Indian actress and model
  - Christian Lindner, German politician
- January 8 – Stipe Pletikosa, Croatian football goalkeeper
- January 9
  - Jake Shields, UFC fighter
  - Tomiko Van, Japanese singer (Do As Infinity)
- January 10
  - Chris Smith, African-American rapper (Kris Kross)
  - James Lloyd, British actor
- January 11 – Siti Nurhaliza, Malaysian singer
- January 12
  - Marián Hossa, Slovak ice hockey player
  - Lee Bo-young, South Korean actress and model
  - Grzegorz Rasiak, Polish footballer
- January 14 – Angela Lindvall, American model
- January 15
  - Drew Brees, American football player
  - Martin Petrov, Bulgarian footballer
- January 16 – Aaliyah, African-American R&B singer and actress (d. 2001)
- January 17 – Sharon Chan, Hong Kong actress
- January 18
  - Jay Chou, Taiwanese singer, song producer and actor
  - Paulo Ferreira, Portuguese footballer
- January 20
  - Asaka Kubo, Japanese gravure idol
  - Will Young, English singer
- January 21 – Brian O'Driscoll, Irish rugby union player
- January 23 – Larry Hughes, American basketball player
- January 24 – Tatyana Ali, African-American actress
- January 27
  - Daniel Vettori, New Zealand cricketer

- ○ Rosamund Pike, British actress
- January 29 – B. J. Flores, American boxer
- January 31 – Jenny Wolf, German speed skater

February

Valentín Elizalde

Irina Slutskaya

Brandy Norwood

Jennifer Love Hewitt

Zhang Ziyi

- February 1
  - Julie Augustyniak, American footballer
  - Peter Fulton, New Zealand cricketer
  - Valentín Elizalde, Mexican singer (d. 2006)
- February 2
  - Yuichi Tsuchiya, Japanese actor
  - Fani Chalkia, Greek athlete
  - Mayer Hawthorne, American soul singer
  - Shamita Shetty, Indian actress and an interior designer
- February 5 – Katie Brambley, Canadian distance freestyle swimmer
- February 6 – David Dolníček, Czech ice hockey player
- February 7 – Michał Karwan, Polish footballer
- February 8 – Martin Rowlands, Irish footballer
- February 9
  - Zhang Ziyi, Chinese actress and model
  - Irina Slutskaya, Russian figure skater
- February 10 – Daryl Palumbo, American musician; who fronted bands, such as (Glassjaw)
- February 11 – Brandy Norwood, African-American singer and actress
- February 12
  - Antonio Chatman, American football player
  - Jesse Spencer, Australian actor
- February 13
  - Anders Behring Breivik, Norwegian right-wing militant
  - Mena Suvari, American actress
  - Rafael Márquez, Mexican footballer
- February 14 – Jocelyn Quivrin, French actor (d. 2009)
- February 15 – Gordon Shedden, Scottish race car driver
- February 16
  - Valentino Rossi, Italian motorcycle racer
  - Eric Mun, leader of Korean boy-band Shinhwa
- February 18 – Tyrone Burton, American actor
- February 19
  - Mariana Ochoa, Mexican singer and actress

- o Vitas, Ukrainian Singer, Model, and Fashion Designer.
- February 21
  - o Carly Colón, Puerto Rican professional wrestler
  - o Christopher Hayes, American Journalist
  - o Jennifer Love Hewitt, American actress and singer
- February 22
  - o Patrick Merrill, Canadian lacrosse player
  - o Maryke Hendrikse, Canadian voice actress
- February 25 – László Bodnár, Hungarian footballer
- February 26
  - o Corinne Bailey Rae, British singer-songwriter and guitarist
  - o Susana Diazayas, Mexican actress
- February 28
  - o Sébastien Bourdais, French racing driver
  - o Sander van Doorn, Dutch DJ and electronic music producer

March

Benji Madden

Joel Madden

Oscar Isaac

Adam Levine

Lee Pace

- March 4
    - Ben Fouhy, New Zealand flatwater canoeist
    - Geoff Huegill, Australian swimmer
    - Jon Fratelli, Scottish singer (The Fratellis)

- March 5 – Tang Gonghong, Chinese weightlifter
- March 6 – Érik Bédard, Canadian pitcher
- March 7 – Stephanie Anne Mills, Canadian voice actress
- March 8
  - Tom Chaplin, British singer (Keane)
  - Jessica Jaymes, American porn actress
- March 9
  - Melina Perez, American professional wrestler
  - Oscar Isaac, American actor
- March 11 – Benji Madden and Joel Madden, American musicians (Good Charlotte)
- March 12 – Pete Doherty, British singer and guitarist (The Libertines, Babyshambles)
- March 14
  - Nicolas Anelka, French footballer
  - Gao Ling, Chinese badminton player
  - Chris Klein, American actor
- March 15 – Kevin Youkilis, American baseball player
- March 17 – Samoa Joe, American wrestler
- March 18
  - Shola Ama, English singer
  - Adam Levine, American singer (Maroon 5)
- March 19
  - Emil Dimitriev, Macedonian politician, Prime Minister
  - Hedo Türkoğlu, Turkish basketball player
- March 20
  - Freema Agyeman, British actress
  - Molly Jenson, American musician
  - Bianca Lawson, American actress
- March 21 – Jimenez Lai, American architect
- March 23 – Bryan Fletcher, American football player
- March 25
  - Lee Pace, American actor
  - Traxamillion, American producer rapper
  - Gorilla Zoe, American rapper
- March 29 – Estela Giménez, Spanish gymnast

- March 30
  - Norah Jones, American musician
  - Simon Webbe, English singer (Blue)

April

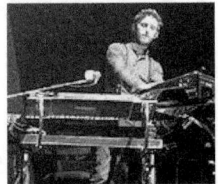

Jesse Carmichael

Claire Danes

Luke Evans

Kourtney Kardashian

Kate Hudson

James McAvoy

Jaime King

- April 1 – Mikko Franck, Finnish conductor
- April 2 – Jesse Carmichael, American musician (Maroon 5)
- April 3
    - Grégoire, French singer-songwriter
    - Živilė Balčiūnaitė, Lithuanian long-distance runner
- April 4
    - Heath Ledger, Australian actor (d. 2008)
    - Roberto Luongo, Canadian ice hockey goaltender
- April 8
    - Tom Kurzanski, American comic artist
    - Alexi Laiho, Finnish rock guitarist (Children of Bodom)
- April 9
    - Keshia Knight Pulliam, African-American actress
    - Mario Matt, Austrian alpine skier
    - Ben Silverstone, British actor
- April 10
    - Rachel Corrie, American activist (d. 2003)
    - Tsuyoshi Domoto, Japanese entertainer (KinKi Kids)
    - Sophie Ellis-Bextor, British singer
- April 11
    - Michel Riesen, Swiss ice hockey player
    - Sebastien Grainger, Canadian singer and musician

- April 12
  - Claire Danes, American actress
  - Jennifer Morrison, American actress
- April 13
  - Baron Davis, American basketball player
  - Tony Lundon, Irish singer (Liberty X)
- April 14
  - Pierre Roland, Indonesian actor
  - Rebecca DiPietro, American model
- April 15 – Luke Evans, Welsh actor and singer
- April 16 – Christijan Albers, Dutch racing driver
- April 17 – Sung Si-kyung, South Korean pop/ballad singer
- April 18
  - Kourtney Kardashian, American reality television star
  - Michael Bradley, American basketball player
  - Yusuke Kamiji, Japanese actor
  - Anthony Davidson, English racing driver
- April 19
  - Kate Hudson, American actress
  - Antoaneta Stefanova, Bulgarian chess player
- April 21 – James McAvoy, Scottish actor
- April 22 – Daniel Johns, Australian musician (Silverchair)
- April 23
  - Lauri Ylönen, Finnish singer (The Rasmus)
  - Jaime King, American actress
  - Yana Gupta, Indian actress of Czech origin
- April 24 – Laurentia Tan, Singaporean Paralympic equestrienne
- April 25
  - Andreas Küttel, Swiss ski jumper
  - Andrea Osvárt, Hungarian actress
- April 26 – Janne Wirman, Finnish keyboardist (Children of Bodom)
- April 27 – Travis Meeks, American musician (Days of the New)
- April 28 – Bahram Radan, Iranian actor
- April 29
  - Jo O'Meara, English singer (S Club 7)

- ○ Matt Tong, drummer (Bloc Party)
- April 30 – Shelley Calene-Black, American voice actress

May

Lance Bass

Jon Montgomery

Rosario Dawson

Mickey Madden

- May 1 – Mauro Bergamasco, Italian rugby union player
- May 2 – Jason Chimera, Canadian ice hockey player
- May 3 – Danny Foster, English singer (Hear'Say)
- May 4
    - Wes Butters, English broadcaster
    - Lance Bass, American singer ('N Sync)
- May 5 – Vincent Kartheiser, American actor
- May 6
    - Mark Burrier, American cartoonist
    - Kerry Ellis, English stage actress/singer
    - Gerd Kanter, Estonian discus thrower
    - Jon Montgomery, Canadian former skeleton racer and television personality; host of The Amazing Race Canada
- May 9
    - Rosario Dawson, African-American actress
    - Pierre Bouvier, Canadian musician
- May 10 – Lee Hyori, South Korean entertainer
- May 12 – Adrian Serioux, Canadian soccer player
- May 13
    - Mickey Madden, American musician (Maroon 5)
    - Carl Philip, Prince of Sweden
- May 14 – Urijah Faber, WEC Featherweight Champion
- May 15 – Ryan Max Riley, humorist and national champion skier

- May 16 – Jessica Morris, American actress
- May 18 – Mariusz Lewandowski, Polish footballer
- May 19
  - Andrea Pirlo, Italian footballer
  - Diego Forlán, Uruguayan football player
- May 22 – Maggie Q, American actress
- May 23 – Matt Flynn, drummer for the alternative band, Maroon 5
- May 24
  - Frank Mir, American mixed martial artist
  - Tracy McGrady, American basketball player
- May 25 – Jonny Wilkinson, English rugby union player
- May 26 – Ashley Massaro, American wrestler and model
- May 27 – Michael Buonauro, American comic creator
- May 28 – Jesse Bradford, American actor
- May 29 – Brian Kendrick, American wrestler
- May 30
  - Mike Bishai, Canadian ice hockey player
  - Clint Bowyer, American race car driver
  - Rie Kugimiya, Japanese voice actress and singer

June

Pete Wentz

Chris Pratt

Ryan Tedder

Felicia Day

- June 4 – Christopher Dorner, American soldier, policeman and multiple murderer (d. 2013)
- June 5 – Pete Wentz, American musician, lyricist, and bassist (Fall Out Boy)
- June 8 – Pete Orr, Canadian baseball player
- June 9 – Émilie Loit, French tennis player
- June 10 – Lee Brice, American country music singer-songwriter
- June 12
  - Amandine Bourgeois, French singer
  - Dallas Clark, American football player
  - Diego Milito, Argentine football player
  - Jodie Prenger, British actress
  - Robyn, Swedish singer-songwriter
- June 13
  - Nila Håkedal, Norwegian beach volleyball player
  - Ágnes Csomor, Hungarian actress
- June 14 – Paradorn Srichaphan, Thai tennis player
- June 15 – Yulia Nestsiarenka, Belarusian athlete
- June 16 – Ari Hest, American singer-songwriter
- June 18
  - Yumiko Kobayashi, Japanese voice actress
  - Chris Neil, Canadian ice hockey player
  - Ivana Wong, Hong Kong singer-songwriter
- June 19
  - John Duddy, Irish boxer
  - Kate Tsui, Hong Kong actress
- June 21 – Chris Pratt, American actor
- June 22 – Sandra Klösel, German tennis player
- June 23 – LaDainian Tomlinson, American football player
- June 24
  - Petra Němcová, Czech model
  - Craig Shergold, British cancer patient
- June 25 – Busy Philipps, American film actress
- June 26 – Ryan Tedder, American singer (OneRepublic), songwriter and producer
-

- June 28
  - Felicia Day, American actress, writer, director, violinist, and singer
  - Randy McMichael, American football player
- June 29
  - Abz Love, English singer (5ive)
  - Marleen Veldhuis, Dutch swimmer
- June 30
  - Rick Gonzalez, American actor
  - Faisal Shahzad, Pakistani-American bomber

July

Kevin Hart

Rose Byrne

- July 1 – Forrest Griffin, American mixed martial arts fighter
- July 2
  - Diana Gurtskaya, Georgian singer
  - Sam Hornish, Jr., American race car driver
  - Ayiesha Woods, American singer
- July 3
  - Sayuri Katayama, Japanese actress, singer and lyricist
  - Ludivine Sagnier, French model and actress
- July 5
  - Shane Filan, Irish singer (Westlife)
  - Amélie Mauresmo, French tennis player
- July 6 – Kevin Hart, American actor, comedian, writer and producer
- July 9
  - Gary Chaw, Malaysian Chinese singer
  - Ella Koon, Hong Kong actress
- July 14 – Axel Teichmann, German cross-country skier
- July 15 – Travis Fimmel, Australian fashion model and actor
- July 16
  - Jayma Mays, American actress and singer
  - Kinya Kotani, Japanese singer
- July 17 – Mike Vogel, American actor
- July 18
  - Rick Baxter, American politician
  - Jaska Raatikainen, Finnish drummer (Children of Bodom)
- July 20
  - Milan Nikolić, Serbian accordionist
  - Amr Shabana, Egyptian squash player
- July 21 – David Carr, American football player
- July 24
  - Rose Byrne, Australian actress
  - Lee Si-yeon, South Korean actress
  - Stat Quo, American rapper
- July 25 – Allister Carter, English snooker player
- July 26
  - Johnson Beharry, British recipient of the Victoria Cross

- o Tamyra Gray, American singer
- o Derek Paravicini, British pianist
- o Peter Sarno, Canadian ice hockey player
- o Mageina Tovah, American actress
- July 27
  - o Jorge Arce, Mexican boxer
  - o Shannon Moore, American professional wrestler
- July 30
  - o Show Luo, Taiwanese singer
  - o Graeme McDowell, Northern Irish professional golfer
  - o Maya Nasser, Syrian journalist (d. 2012)

August

Jason Momoa

Evangeline Lilly

Aaron Paul

Maria Haukaas Mittet

- August 1
  - Jason Momoa, American actor
  - Honeysuckle Weeks, British actress
- August 3
  - Evangeline Lilly, Canadian actress
  - Maria Haukaas Mittet, Norwegian recording artist
- August 5 – David Healy, Northern Irish footballer
- August 4 – Patryk Dominik Sztyber, Polish metal musician
- August 7 – Miguel Llera, Spanish footballer
- August 8 – Azumi Kawashima, Japanese idol and AV idol
- August 10
  - Joanna García, American actress
  - Ted Geoghegan, American screenwriter
  -

- August 11
  - Drew Nelson, Canadian actor and voice actor
  - Bubba Crosby, American baseball player
- August 12 – Cindy Klassen, Canadian speed skater
- August 13 – Taizō Sugimura, Japanese politician
- August 15
  - Carl Edwards, American race car driver
  - Dan Marshall, Canadian hockey player
  - Peter Shukoff, American comedian, musician and personality
- August 16 – Sarah Balabagan, Filipina prisoner and singer
- August 19 – Oumar Kondé, Swiss footballer
- August 20 – Jamie Cullum, English jazz pianist and singer
- August 22 – Matt Walters, American football player
- August 23 – Ritchie Neville, English singer (5ive)
- August 24 – Elva Hsiao, Taiwanese singer
- August 25 – Andrew Hussie, American artist.
- August 26
  - Jamal Lewis, American football player
  - Cristian Mora, Ecuadorian footballer
- August 27
  - Giovanni Capitello, American filmmaker/actor
  - Tian Liang, Chinese diver
  - Aaron Paul, American actor
- August 28
  - Robert Hoyzer, German football referee
  - Yuki Maeda, Japanese singer
- August 29 – Justine Pasek, Miss Universe 2002
- August 30
  - Tavia Yeung, Hong Kong actress
  - Niki Chow, Hong Kong actress
- August 31
  - Mickie James, American professional wrestler
  - Simon Neil, Scottish musician (vocalist, guitarist, songwriter), Biffy Clyro Marmaduke Duke
  - Yuvan Shankar Raja, Indian film composer

September

Peter Browngardt

Bam Margera

Pink

Flo Rida

Jing Jong-oh

- September 1 – Neg Dupree, British comedian
- September 2
  - Ron Ng, Hong Kong actor
  - Łukasz Żygadło, Polish volleyball player
- September 3 – Júlio César, Brazilian football goalkeeper
- September 4 – Maxim Afinogenov, Russian ice hockey player
- September 5
  - John Carew, Norwegian footballer
  - Stacey Dales, Canadian basketball player and sportscaster
- September 6 – Ned Collette, Australian singer and musician
- September 8 – Pink, American singer
- September 10 – Mustis, Norwegian pianist
- September 11
  - Ariana Richards, American actress
  - Éric Abidal, French footballer
- September 12
  - Jay McGraw, American author, son of TV psychologist Dr. Phil McGraw
  - Peter Browngardt, American cartoonist
- September 13 – Ivan Miljković, Serbian volleyball player
- September 14
  - Stuart Fielden, English rugby league player
  - Kamya Panjabi, Indian television actress
  -

- September 15
  - Amy Davidson, American actress
  - Edna Ngeringway Kiplagat, Kenyan long-distance runner
- September 16
  - Fanny, French singer
  - Flo Rida, African-American rapper
- September 17 – Akin Ayodele, American football player
  - Chuck Comeau, Canadian drummer
- September 18 – Alison Lohman, American actress
- September 19 – Noémie Lenoir, French supermodel
- September 20 – David Long, New Zealand musician
- September 22 – Jericho Rosales, Filipino actor
- September 23 – Lote Tuqiri, Australian rugby union player
- September 24
  - Justin Bruening, American actor and model
  - Erin Chambers, American actress
  - Jing Jong-oh, Korean shooting
- September 25 – Rashad Evans, a fighter in the MMA sport UFC
- September 26
  - Naomichi Marufuji, Japanese professional wrestler
  - Taavi Rõivas, Prime Minister of Estonia
- September 27 – Shinji Ono, Japanese football player
- September 28
  - Bam Margera, American skateboarder
  - Dane Boedigheimer (Daneboe), American YouTuber and animator
- September 29
  - Gaitana, Ukrainian singer and songwriter of Ukrainian and Congolese descent
  - Artika Sari Devi, Putri Indonesia 2004
- September 30 – Vince Chong, Malaysian singer

October

Chris O'Dowd

Brandon Routh

John Krasinski

- October 1
  - Rudi Johnson, American football player
  - Senit, Italian singer of Eritrean descent
  - Marko Stanojevic, English-born Italian rugby union player
- October 2 – Brianna Brown, American actress
- October 3
  - Matt Davis, American stand-up comedian
  - John Hennigan, American professional wrestler
  - Danny O'Donoghue, Irish singer-songwriter (The Script)
- October 4 – Rachael Leigh Cook, American actress
- October 5 – Gao Yuanyuan, Chinese actress
- October 7
  - Simona Amanar, Romanian gymnast
  - Susan Eldridge, American supermodel
  - Tang Wei, Chinese actress
- October 9
  - Csézy, Hungarian singer
  - Vernon Fox, American football player
  - Alex Greenwald, American singer-songwriter, producer, and actor (Phantom Planet and JJAMZ)
  - Todd Kelly, Australian race car driver
  - Chris O'Dowd, Irish actor and comedian
  - DJ Rashad, Chicago-based electronic musician, producer and DJ (d. 2014)
  - Hendrik Odendaal, South African swimmer
  - Brandon Routh, American actor
  - Gonzalo Sorondo, Uruguayan footballer
- October 10
  - Wu Chun, Bruneian actor, model, and singer
  - Nicolás Massú, Chilean tennis player
  - Mýa, American singer and actress
- October 11
  - Bae Doona, South Korean actress
  - Gabe Saporta, Uruguayan singer (Cobra Starship)
- October 13
  - Ryan Malcolm, Canadian singer

- ○ Mamadou Niang, Senegalese footballer
- October 14 – Stacy Keibler, American actress and model
- October 15 – Jaci Velasquez, American Christian singer
- October 16 – Erin Brown, American actress
- October 17 – Kimi Räikkönen, Finnish race car driver
- October 18 – Ne-Yo, African-American singer and songwriter
- October 19 – Marc Elliott, British actor
- October 20
  - ○ John Krasinski, American actor
  - ○ Paul O'Connell, Irish rugby union player
- October 23 – Jorge Solís, Mexican professional boxer
- October 28_ Jawed Karim; Co-founder of Youtube
  - ○ Brett Dennen, American folk/pop singer and songwriter
  - ○ Martin Škoula, Czech ice hockey player
- October 30 – Yukie Nakama, Japanese actress

November

Lamar Odom

Joel Kinnaman

- November 1
  - Coco Crisp, American baseball player
  - Atsuko Enomoto, Japanese voice actress
  - Milan Dudić, Serbian footballer
- November 3
  - Pablo Aimar, Argentine footballer
  - Tim McIlrath, American rock singer, songwriter (Rise Against)
- November 4 – Audrey Hollander, American pornographic actress
- November 6
  - Lamar Odom, African-American retired basketball player
  - Myolie Wu, Hong Kong actress
- November 7 – Jon Peter Lewis, American singer and songwriter
- November 8
  - Aaron Hughes, Northern Irish footballer
  - Salvatore Cascio, Italian actor (Cinema Paradiso)
- November 9 – Dania Ramirez, Dominican-American actress
- November 12
  - Cote de Pablo, Chilean actress
  - Matt Stevic, Australian rules football umpire
- November 13 – Metta World Peace, American basketball player
- November 14
  - Mavie Hörbiger, German actress
  - Olga Kurylenko, Ukrainian model and actress
  - Mpule Kwelagobe, Miss Universe 1999

- November 17 – Matthew Spring, English footballer
- November 19 – Larry Johnson, American football player
- November 20 – Ericson Alexander Molano, Colombian gospel singer
- November 21 – Kim Dong-wan, South Korean singer and actor
- November 22
    - Chris Doran, Irish singer
    - Scott Robinson, English singer (5ive)
- November 23
    - Ivica Kostelić, Croatian alpine skier
    - Kelly Brook, English actress/model
- November 25 – Joel Kinnaman, Swedish-American actor
- November 27
    - Ricky Carmichael, American motorcycle and stock car racer
    - Hilary Hahn, American violinist
- November 28
    - Dane Bowers, English singer-songwriter (Another Level)
    - Jamie Korab, Canadian curler
    - Hakeem Seriki, African-American rapper (Chamillionaire)
- November 29 – Jayceon Taylor, American rapper (The Game)

December

Sabina Babayeva

Sara Bareilles

Rider Strong

Mihai Trăistariu

Adam Brody

- December 2
  - Sabina Babayeva, Azerbaijani singer
  - Yvonne Catterfeld, German singer
- December 3
  - Daniel Bedingfield, English pop singer and songwriter
  - Rock Cartwright, American football player
  - Rainbow Sun Francks, Canadian actor and singer
- December 5 – Evonne Hsu, Taiwanese singer
- December 7
  - Jennifer Carpenter, American actress
  - Eric Bauza, Canadian comedian and voice actor
  - Sara Bareilles, American singer, songwriter and pianist
  - Ayako Fujitani, Japanese actress
- December 8 – Ingrid Michaelson, American indie pop singer-songwriter
- December 9 – Olivia Lufkin, English-Japanese singer, songwriter
- December 11 – Rider Strong, American actor
- December 12 – Emin, Azerbaijani-Russian singer-songwriter and businessman
- December 14 – Michael Owen, English footballer
- December 15 – Adam Brody, American actor
- December 16
  - Mihai Trăistariu, Romanian singer and musician
  - Trevor Immelman, South African golfer
- December 17
  - William Green, American football player
  - Matt Murley, American hockey player

- December 18 – Amy Grabow, American actress
- December 19
  - Kevin Devine, American songwriter and musician
  - Paola Rey, Colombian actress and model
- December 22
  - Petra Majdič, Slovene cross-country skier
  - Amanda Baker, American actress
- December 23
  - Summer Altice, American model and actress
  - Kenny Miller, Scottish football player
- December 25 – Ferman Akgül, vocalist of Turkish nu-metal band maNga
- December 26
  - Chris Daughtry, American singer and guitarist
  - Dimitry Vassiliev, Russian ski jumper
- December 27 – Carson Palmer, American football player
- December 28
  - James Blake, American tennis pro
  - Diego Luna, Mexican actor
  - Robert Edward Davis, German-American rapper
- December 30
  - Milana Terloeva, Chechen journalist and author
  - Yelawolf, American rapper
- December 31
  - Bob Bryar, American drummer (My Chemical Romance)
  - Elaine Cassidy, Irish actress

Deaths

January

Nelson Rockefeller

- January 3 – Conrad Hilton, American hotelier (b. 1887)
- January 4 – Vincent Korda, Hungarian art director (b. 1897)
- January 4 – Peter Frankenfeld, German comedian, radio and television personality (b. 1913)
- January 5
  - Billy Bletcher, American actor (b. 1894)
  - Charles Mingus, American musician (b. 1922)
- January 7 – Wallace Townsend, Iowa-born lawyer who was from 1928 to 1961 the Republican national committeeman (b. 1882)
- January 8 – Sara Carter, American bluegrass and country singer (b. 1898)
- January 11 – Jack Soo, Japanese-American actor (b. 1917)
- January 13 – Donny Hathaway, African-American musician (b. 1945)
- January 16
  - Peter Butterworth, English actor (b. 1919)
  - Ted Cassidy, American actor (b. 1932)
- January 19 – Tuffy Leemans, American football player (New York Giants) and a member of the Pro Football Hall of Fame (b. 1912)
- January 22 – Elvin C. Stakman, American plant pathologist (b. 1885)

- January 25 – Robertson Hare, English actor (b. 1891)
- January 26 – Nelson Rockefeller, Governor of New York, Vice President of the United States (b. 1908)
- January 27 – Qalandar Baba Auliya, Pakistani founder of the Azeemiyya Order of the Sufis (b. 1898)
- January 28 – Glen Flanagan, American featherweight boxer (b. 1926)
- January 29
  - Alf Ahlberg, Swedish writer, humanist, and philosopher (b. 1892)
  - Andy Harrington (pinch hitter), American professional baseball player (b. 1903)
- January 30 – Charles Watts (cricketer, born 1894), English cricketer (b. 1894)

February

- February 1 – Daniel Starch, American psychologist and marketing researcher (b. 1883)
- February 2
  - Issa Pliyev, Soviet general (b. 1903)
  - Sid Vicious, English musician (*Sex Pistols*) (drug overdose) (b. 1957)
- February 3 – Aaron Douglas, American painter (b. 1899)
- February 4 – Claude Massop, Jamaican gang leader of the Shower Posse Gang (b. c. 1949)
- February 5 – Reidar Waaler, Norwegian-born, American soldier for the United States Army (b. 1894)
- February 6 – Mary Bell (aviator), Australian aviator (b. 1903)
- February 7
  - Warren Giles, Major League Baseball executive and commissioner from 1951 to 1969; National Baseball Hall of Fame inductee in 1979 (b. 1896)
  - Josef Mengele, German Nazi war criminal (b. 1911)
  - Elizabeth O'Neill Verner, artist, author and lecturer from Charleston, South Carolina (b. 1883)

- February 8 – Art Williams (umpire), African-American baseball umpire (b. 1934)
- February 9 – Dennis Gabor, Hungarian physicist, Nobel Prize laureate (b. 1900)
- February 10 – Edvard Kardelj, Yugoslav communist political leader, economist, partisan and publicist (b. 1910)
- February 12 – Jean Renoir, French film director (b. 1894)
- February 14 – Reginald Maudling, British politician (b. 1917)
- February 15 – George Dunning, cartoon director and animator (b. 1920)
- February 17 – William Gargan, American actor (b. 1905)
- February 22 – Sigrid Schauman, Finnish painter (b. 1877)
- February 23 – W. A. C. Bennett, Canadian politician (b. 1900)
- February 24 – Joseph Rudderham, English prelate of the Roman Catholic Church (b. 1899)
- February 25 – Henrich Focke, German aviation pioneer (b. 1890)
- February 26 – Devendra Goel, Indian film director and producer of Bollywood films (b. 1919)
- February 27
  - John F. Seitz, American Academy Award-nominated cinematographer (b. 1892)
  - Hanns-Horst von Necker, German Nazi Generalmajor in the Luftwaffe; highly decorated (b. 1903)
- February 28 – Ethel Remey, American actress (b. 1895)

March

- March 1
  - Mustafa Barzani, Iraqi Kurdish politician (b. 1903)
  - Dolores Costello, American actress (b. 1903)
- March 6 – Link Wasem, American baseball player (b. 1911)
- March 10 – William Boyd (pathologist), Scottish-Canadian physician, pathologist, academic, and author (b. 1885)
- March 11 – Victor Kilian, American actor (b. 1891)
- March 14 – Robert William Wood, American landscape painter (b. 1889)

- March 15 – Léonide Massine, Russian dancer and choreographer (b. 1896)
- March 16 – Jean Monnet, French political economist and diplomat (b. 1888)
- March 16 – Carmen de Icaza, Spanish writer (b. 1899)
- March 17 – Alfred Brotherston Emden, Oxford University historian and Principal of St Edmund Hall from 1929 to 1951.(b. 1888)
- March 19 – Richard Beckinsale, British actor (b. 1947)
- March 22 – Ben Lyon, American actor (b. 1901)
- March 23 – Ted Anderson, English footballer (b. 1911)
- March 24 – Yvonne Mitchell, English actress (b. 1915)
- March 26 – Jean Stafford, American writer (b. 1915)
- March 28 – Emmett Kelly, American clown (b. 1898)
- March 29 – Sultan Yahya Petra ibni Almarhum Sultan Ibrahim Petra, King of Malaysia (b. 1917)
- March 30
    - Airey Neave, British politician (assassinated) (b. 1916)
    - José María Velasco Ibarra, former President of Ecuador (b. 1893)

April

Zulfikar Ali Bhutto

Phan Huy Quat

- April 1 – Barbara Luddy, American actress (b. 1908)
- April 2 – Grace Fortescue, New York socialite (b. 1883)
- April 4
  - Zulfikar Ali Bhutto, President and Prime Minister of Pakistan (executed) (b. 1928)
  - Edgar Buchanan, American actor (b. 1903)
- April 6 – Ivan Vasilyov, Bulgarian architect (b. 1893)
- April 7
  - Frank J. Donahue, American politician (b. 1881)
  - Charles W. Sawyer, United States Secretary of Commerce (b. 1887)
- April 10 – Nino Rota, Italian composer (b. 1911)
- April 11 – Hassan Pakravan, Iranian diplomat (b. 1911)
- April 13 – Frankie Kelleher, American baseball player (b. 1916)
- April 14 – Clarence Dillon, American financier (b.1882)
- April 15 – David Brand, Australian politician (b. 1912)
- April 17 – Chuck Osborne, American basketball player with Syracuse Nationals (b. 1939)
- April 18 – Jullan Kindahl, Swedish actress (b. 1885)
- April 19 – Wilhelm Bittrich, German *Waffen SS* general (b. 1894)
- April 20 – Peter Donald, British-born, American actor (b. 1918)
- April 22 – Leslie Phillips (cricketer), English cricketer (b. 1899)
- April 23 – Blair Peach, New Zealand-born, British teacher (b. 1946)
- April 24 – John Carroll, American actor (b. 1906)
- April 26 – Julia Bell, English human geneticist (b. 1879)

- April 27 – Phan Huy Quát, Vietnamese physician, acting Prime Minister of the State of Vietnam, and Prime Minister of the Republic of Vietnam (b. c. 1909)
- April 28 – Norman Kilner, English cricketer (b. 1895)
- April 30 – Pan Halippa, Bessarabian and later Romanian journalist and politician (b. 1883)

May

Giulio Natta

Barbara Hutton

Paul Southwell

Mary Pickford

- May 1 – Morteza Motahhari, Iranian cleric & politician (b. 1919)
- May 2 – Giulio Natta, Italian chemist, Nobel Prize laureate (b. 1903)
- May 3
    - John Field (American football), American football player and corset & lingerie manufacturer (b. 1886)
    - Gordon Luce, British manuscript, book, and photograph collector (b. 1889)
- May 4 – John Bentley Stringer, British computer scientist (b. 1928)
- May 6 – Milton Ager, American songwriter (b. 1893)
- May 7 – Ralph Huffman, American college football coach for the Fort Hays State University Tigers (b. 1915)

- May 8 – Victor Saville, American film director and producer (b. 1895)
- May 9 – Cyrus S. Eaton, Canadian-born American investment banker, businessman and philanthropist (b. 1883)
- May 10 – Ita Rina, Slovenian film actress & beauty queen (b. 1907)
- May 11
  - Joan Chandler, American actress (b. 1923)
  - Lester Flatt, American bluegrass and folk singer (b. 1914)
  - Barbara Hutton, American socialite (b. 1912)
- May 12
  - Rosario María Gutiérrez Eskildsen, Méxican lexicographer (b. 1899)
  - Clyde Kluttz, American baseball player, scout, and executive (b. 1917)
- May 13
  - Predrag Đajić, Bosnian Serb and Yugoslav footballer (b. 1922)
  - Iris Hoey, British actress (b. 1885)
- May 14 – Jean Rhys, mid-20th-century novelist from Dominica.(b. 1890)
- May 16
  - Robert Florey, French-American film director and screenwriter,(b. 1900)
  - Margaret Harwood, American astronomer and the first Director of the Maria Mitchell Observatory in Nantucket, Massachusetts (b. 1885)
  - A. Philip Randolph, African-American civil rights leader (b. 1889)
- May 17 – Donyale Luna, First African-American model who appeared on the cover of *Vogue* in March 1966 (b. 1945)
- May 18
  - Volodymyr Ivasyuk, Ukrainian songwriter, composer, and poet (b. 1949)
  - Paul Southwell, Premier and First Minister of Saint Kitts and Nevis (b. 1913)

- May 19 – Hazari Prasad Dwivedi, Hindi novelist (b. 1907)
- May 20 – Helen Smith (nurse), British nurse (b. 1956)
- May 22 – Kurt Jooss, German dancer and choreographer (b. 1901)
- May 23 – Hiroshi Ohshita, Japanese professional baseball player (b. 1922)
- May 24 – Albert W. Cretella, U. S. Representative from Connecticut (b. 1897)
- May 25 – John Spenkelink, American convicted murderer (b. 1949)
- May 25 – American Airlines Flight 191 Casualties
  - Itzhak Bentov, Czech-born, Israeli-American scientist, inventor, and author (b. 1923)
    - Other notable deaths: Sheila Charisse; daughter-in-law of Cyd Charisse, Leonard Stogel - a band manager, promoter, & executive for such band as: The Cowsills & Tommy James & The Shondells, Victoria Haider - *Playboy* magazine editor, Judith & Sheldon Wax - Judith; an editor contributor and Sheldon; a managing editor for *Playboy*, Robert Walton Vaughan - Professor of Chemical Engineering at the California Institute of Technology.
- May 26 – George Brent, Irish actor (b. 1899)
- May 27
  - Margot Benary-Isbert, German writer (b. 1889)
  - Ahmed Ould Bouceif, Mauritanian military leader (b. 1934)
- May 28 – Frank Frederickson, Canadian NHL hockey player (b. 1895)
- May 29 – Mary Pickford, Canadian Academy Award-winning actress and studio founder (b. 1892)
- May 31
  - Marcel Merminod, Swiss film actor (b. 1893)
  - Scott Vincent, American radio & television announcer and news anchor (b. 1922)

June

Werner Forssmann

John Wayne

- June 1
  - ○ Werner Forssmann, German physician, recipient of the Nobel Prize in Physiology or Medicine (b. 1904)
  - ○ Ján Kadár, Czechoslovakian film director (b. 1918)
  - ○ Jack Mulhall, American actor (b. 1887)
- June 2 – Jim Hutton, American actor (b. 1934)
- June 3 – Arno Schmidt, German writer (b. 1914)
- June 4
  - ○ Lazar Lagin, Soviet satirical and children's writer (b.1903)
  - ○ Neville Alexander Odartey-Wellington, Ghanaian army officer (b. 1934)

- June 5 – Heinz Erhardt, German comedian, musician, entertainer, actor, and poet (b. 1909)
- June 6 – Jack Haley, American actor (b. 1898)
- June 7 – Asa Earl Carter, American novellist (b. 1925)
- June 8 – Muriel Coben, Canadian baseball and curling player (b. 1921)
- June 9
  - Scott Garland (ice hockey), Canadian ice hockey player (b. 1952)
  - Cyclone Taylor, Canadian ice hockey player (b. 1884)
- June 10 – Winifred Mary Ward, the sister of Francis Kingdon Ward.(b. 1884)
- June 11
  - Edward Almond, American general (b. 1892)
  - John Wayne, American Academy Award-winning actor (*The Searchers*; *True Grit*) (b. 1907)
- June 12
  - Bill Brenzel, American Major League Baseball catcher (b. 1910)
  - Constant Joacim, Belgian footballer (b. 1908)
- June 13
  - George Cisar, American actor (b. 1912)
  - Darla Hood, American actress (b. 1931)
- June 14 – Ahmad Zahir, Afghan singer and composer (b. 1946)
- June 15 – Laurie Bird, American actress (b. 1952)
- June 16 – Nicholas Ray, American film director (b. 1911)
- June 17 – Duffy Lewis, American baseball player (b. 1888)
- June 18 – Hal Trosky, American baseball player (b 1912)
- June 19 – Paul Popenoe, American eugenicist (b. 1888)
- June 21 – Angus MacLise, American rock percussionist (The Velvet Underground) (b. 1938)
- June 22
  - Louis Chiron, Monacan Grand Prix driver (b. 1899)
  - Hope Summers, American actress (b. 1896)
- June 23 – Cremilda de Oliveira, Portuguese actress (b. 1887)
- June 25 – Dave Fleischer, American animator (b. 1894)

- June 26 – George Boakye, Ghanaian Military airman and politician (b. 1937)
- June 27
  - Ludovico Arroyo Bañas, Philippines Telecommications official (b. 1901)
  - Pat Maloney, American baseball plyar (b. 1887)
- June 28 – Philippe Cousteau, French oceanographer, and documentary filmmaker (b. 1940)
- June 29 – Lowell George, American rock musician (*Little Feat*) (b. 1945)
- June 30 – William B. Franke, American United States Secretary of the Navy from (1959-1961) (b.1894)

July

Robert Woodward

Arthur Fiedler

Gustavo Diaz Ordaz

- July 1
  - Douglas McKenzie, Australian cricketer (b. 1906)
  - Richard Ward (actor), gravely-voiced, African-American actor (b. 1915)
- July 2 – Carlyle Smith Beals, Canadian astronomer (b. 1899)
- July 3 – Louis Durey, French composer (b. 1888)
- July 4
  - Frank H. Ellis, Canadian aviator and Member of the Early Birds (b. 1896)
  - Theodora Kroeber, American writer and anthropologist (b. 1897)
  - Marjorie Rhodes, British actress (b. 1897)
  - Mendy Rudolph, American baseketball referee of the NBA (b. 1926)
- July 6 – Van McCoy, African-American accomplished musician; noted for his 1975 hit *The Hustle* (b. 1940)
- July 7 – Billy Dean Anderson, Notorious American criminal on "America's 10 Most Wanted" (b. 1934)
- July 8
  - Elizabeth Ryan, American 30 Grand Slam (tennis) Tennis Champion (b. 1892)

- o Sin-Itiro Tomonaga, Japanese physicist, Nobel Prize laureate (b. 1906)
- o Michael Wilding, English actor (b. 1912)
- o Robert B. Woodward, American chemist, Nobel Prize laureate (b. 1917)
- July 9 – Roddy McMillan, Scottish actor (b. 1923)
- July 10 – Arthur Fiedler, American conductor (*Boston Pops*) (b. 1894)
- July 11
  - o Giorgio Ambrosoli, Italian lawyer (b. 1933)
  - o Else Højgaard, Danish ballerina (b. 1906)
  - o Claude Wagner, French-Canadian judge and Progressive Conservative senator appointed in 1978 (b. 1925)
- July 12 – Minnie Riperton, American R&B singer (*Lovin' You*) (b. 1947)
- July 13
  - o Corinne Griffith, American actress (b. 1894)
  - o Ludwig Merwart, Austrian painter and graphic artist (1913)
- July 14 – McGuire Twins; One of the heaviest recorded twins by Guinness World Records, Billy died. (b. 1946)
- July 15
  - o Gustavo Díaz Ordaz, Mexican President (b. 1911)
  - o Juana de Ibarbourou, Uruguayan poet (b. 1892)
- July 16 – Alfred Deller, English countertenor (b. 1912)
- July 18 – Pavel Prokkonen, Karelian Soviet politician (b. 1909)
- July 19 – Helen Bradley, English artist whose works depicted the Edwardian era (b. 1900)
- July 20 – Volney Davis, American Depression era outlaw (b. 1902)
- July 21 – Juan Guzmán Cruchaga, Chilean poet & diplomat (b. 1895)
- July 22
  - o Tony Galento, American boxer (b. 1910)
  - o Sándor Kocsis, Hungarian footballer (b. 1929)
- July 23 – Lefty West, American Major League Baseball player (b. 1915)
- July 25 – Erich Pohlmann, Austrian character actor (b. 1913)

- July 26 – Stefan Wiechecki, Polish journalist (b. 1896)
- July 27 – Gustavo Cochet, Argentine painter and engraver (b. 1894)
- July 28 – George Seaton, American screenwriter and director (b. 1911)
- July 29
  - Bill Todman, American game show producer (b. 1916)
  - Herbert Marcuse, German American philosopher, sociologist, and political theorist (b. 1898)
- July 30 – Lew Kowarski, Russian-born, French physicist (b. 1907)
- July 31 – Beatrix Lehmann, British actress, theatre director, and author (b. 1903)

August

Ernst Boris Chain

Louis Mountbatten

Jean Seberg

- August 1 – Wayne Brenkert, American football player-coach (b. 1895)
- August 2
  - Víctor Raúl Haya de la Torre, Peruvian politician, founder of the APRA Party (b. 1895)
  - Thurman Munson, American baseball player (b. 1947)
- August 3 – Bertil Ohlin, Swedish economist, Nobel Prize laureate (b. 1899)
- August 4
  - Reynold C. Fuson, American chemist (b. 1895)
  - Roger Lambrecht, Belgian road bicycle rider (b. 1916)
- August 5 – Homero Hidrobo, Ecudorian classical musician (b. 1939)
- August 6 – Feodor Felix Konrad Lynen, German biochemist, recipient of the Nobel Prize in Physiology or Medicine (b. 1911)
- August 7 – Margery Maude, English stage actress (b. 1889)
- August 8
  - Lionel Cooper (mathematician), South African mathematician (b. 1915)
  - George Rider, American basketball coach (b. 1890)
- August 9 – Walter O'Malley, American baseball executive (b. 1903)
- August 10
  - Dick Foran, American actor (b. 1910)
  - Mohammad Nur Ahmad Etemadi, Afghan politician, former Prime Minister (b. 1921)
- August 11
  - Alim Ashirov, Soviet footballer (b. 1955)

- J. G. Farrell, Liverpool-born, Irish novelist (b. 1935)
- August 12 – Ernst Boris Chain, German-born biochemist, recipient of the Nobel Prize in Physiology or Medicine (b. 1906)
- August 13 – Andrew Dasburg, American modernist painter (b. 1887)
- August 15
  - Zygmunt Witymir Bieńkowski, Polish pilot and writer (b. 1913)
  - Asa Martin, American old time musician (b. 1900)
- August 16 – John Diefenbaker, 13th Prime Minister of Canada (b. 1895)
- August 17 – Vivian Vance, American actress (b. 1909)
- August 18 – Draper Kauffman, American Naval pioneering underwater demolition expert (b. 1911)
- August 19
  - Mary Millington, British porn star (b. 1945)
  - Joel Teitelbaum, Hungarian Rebbe (b. 1887)
- August 20 – Christian Dotremont, Belgian painter and writer (b. 1922)
- August 21 – Stuart Heisler, American film and television director (b. 1896)
- August 22 – James T. Farrell, American novelist (b. 1904)
- August 23 – Richard Hearne, English comedic actor (b. 1908)
- August 24 – Hanna Reitsch, German aviator (b. 1912)
- August 25 – Stan Kenton, American jazz pianist (b. 1911)
- August 26 – Alvin Karpis, last of America's depression era criminals (b. 1907)
- August 27 – Louis Mountbatten, 1st Earl Mountbatten of Burma, British Viceroy of India (assassinated) (b. 1900)
- August 28 – Princess Tatiana Constantinovna of Russia, Former Russian royal princess (b. 1890)
- August 29 – Samuel Irving Newhouse, Sr., American media entrepreneur and publisher (b. 1895)
- August 30 (body found on September 8) – Jean Seberg, American actress (b. 1938)
- August 31 – Sally Rand, American dancer (b. 1904)

September

Gracie Fields

- September 1
  - Doris Kenyon, American actress (b. 1897)
  - Stanley R. Mullard, English industrialist (b. 1883)
- September 2 – Felix Aylmer, British actor (b. 1889)
- September 3
  - Lim Cheng Hoe, Chinese-born, Singaporean watercolorist (b. 1912)
  - Wincenty Okołowicz, Polish geographer & climatologist (b. 1906)
  - Juan Pablo Pérez Alfonso, Venezuelan politician (b. 1903)
- September 4 – Canuplin, Filipino magician and bodabil entertainer (b. 1904)
- September 5 – Alberto di Jorio, Italian Roman Catholic cardinal (b. 1884)
- September 6 – Guy Bolton, British playwright (b. 1884)
- September 7 – Alan Browning, English actor (b. 1926)
- September 8
  - Princess Hilda of Luxembourg (1897–1979), Luxembourgian princess (b. 1897)
  - Rick Joseph, Dominican baseball player (b. 1939)
- September 9 – Norrie Paramor, British music producer (b. 1914)
- September 10 – Agostinho Neto, Angolan nationalist (b. 1922)
- September 11 – Laurie Banfield, English footballer (b. 1889)
- September 13 – Hap Ward, American baseball player (b. 1885)

- September 14 – Nur Muhammad Taraki, President of Afghanistan (b. 1917)
- September 15 – Tommy Leonetti, American singer-songwriter & actor (b. 1929)
- September 16
  - Giò Ponti, Italian architect, industrial designer, furniture designer and artist (b. 1891)
  - Rob Slotemaker, Indonesian-born, Dutch Formula 1 racing car driver (b. 1929)
- September 17 – Paul Maze, Anglo-French painter (b. 1887)
- September 18 – André Zeller, French army general (b. 1898)
- September 19
  - Lou Busch, American record producer, singer, and songwriter (b. 1910)
  - Mary Ann Nyberg, American costumer designer (b. 1923)
- September 20
  - Sultan Ismail Nasiruddin Shah, King of Malaysia (b. 1907)
  - Ludvík Svoboda, president of Czechoslovakia (b. 1895)
- September 21
  - Edmund Morgan (bishop), the seventh Suffragan Bishop of Southampton (b. 1888)
  - Bernard L. Austin, American admiral (b. 1902)
- September 22
  - Abul A'la Maududi, Pakistani journalist and philosopher (b. 1903)
  - Otto Robert Frisch, Austrian-British physicist (b. 1904)
- September 23 – Steve Brooks (jockey), American jockey (b. 1922)
- September 24 – Carl Laemmle, Jr., American film studio executive (b. 1908)
- September 25
  - Yury Kovalyov, Soviet footballer (b. 1934)
  - Karl Schnörrer, German Nazi "ace" for the Luftwaffe; nicknamed "Quax" (b. 1919)
- September 26
  - John Cromwell, American film director and actor (b. 1887)
  - Arthur Hunnicutt, American actor (b. 1910)

- September 27
  - Gracie Fields, British actress (b. 1898)
  - Jimmy McCulloch, Scottish guitarist (Paul McCartney & Wings) (b. 1953)
- September 28 – John Herbert Chapman, Canadian physicist (b. 1921)
- September 29 – Francisco Macías Nguema, first president of Equatorial Guinea (executed) (b. 1924)
- September 30 – Charles North (politician), Australian attorney and politician (b. 1887)

October

Park Chung-hee

- October 1
  - Dorothy Arzner, American film director (b. 1897)
  - Roy Harris, American composer (b. 1898)
- October 2
  - Ray Genet, American mountain climber (b. 1931)
  - Hannelore Schmatz, German mountaineer (b. 1940)
- October 3
  - Claudia Jennings, American model (b. 1949)
  - Dorothy Peterson, American film and television actress (b. 1897)
  - Nicos Poulantzas, Greek sociologist (b. 1936)

- October 4 – Natwarsinhji Bhavsinhji, The Maharaja of Porbandar in India from (1908-1948), and cricketer (b. 1901)
- October 5 – Ken Strong, American football player (New York Giants) and a member of the Pro Football Hall of Fame (b. 1906)
- October 6 – Elizabeth Bishop, American poet (b. 1911)
- October 7 – Jerzy Petersburski, Polish pianist & composer (b. 1895)
- October 8 – Emmaline Henry, American actress (b. 1928)
- October 9 – Ignatius Bedros XVI Batanian, Armenian Catholic Church patriarch (b. 1899)
- October 10 – Dr. Christopher Evans, British psychologist and computer scientist (b. 1931)
- October 12
  - Katharine Blodgett, American inventor (b. 1898)
  - Rene Gagnon, U.S. Marine flag raiser on Iwo Jima (b. 1925)
  - Celia Lovsky, Austrian-American actress (b. 1897)
- October 13
  - Rebecca Helferich Clarke, English composer and violist (b. 1886)
  - Clarence Muse, American actor (b. 1889)
  - Archibald Roosevelt, American conservative political activist, son of President Theodore Roosevelt (b. 1894)
- October 14 – Onorato Damen, Italian communist revolutionary (b. 1893)
- October 15 – Jacob L. Devers, American general (b. 1887)
- October 16 – Johan Borgen, Norwegian author (b. 1903)
- October 17 – S. J. Perelman, American humorist (b. 1904)
- October 18
  - Joe Coomer (American football), American football player (b. 1917)
  - Virgilio Piñera, Cuban author, playwright, & poet (b. 1912)
- October 19 – Fritz Diez, German actor (b. 1901)
- October 22 – Nadia Boulanger, French composer and composition teacher (b. 1887)
- October 23
  - Antonio Caggiano, Argentine cardinal (b. 1889)

- o Johann Sinnhuber, German general in the Wehrmacht (b. 1887)
- October 24 – Julio Porter, Argentine screenwriter (b. 1916)
- October 25
  - o Eva Puck, American vaudeville headliner actress (b. 1892)
  - o Gerald Templer, British Army Field Marshal in World War I and World War II (b. 1898)
- October 26
  - o Park Chung-hee, President of South Korea (assassinated) (b. 1917)
  - o Charles P. Thompson, American actor (b. 1891)
- October 27 – Charles Coughlin, American radio host and Catholic Priest, (b. 1891)
- October 28 – Joseph-Henri Guiguet, French World War I flying ace (b. 1891)
- October 30
  - o Barnes Wallis, British aeronautical engineer (b. 1887)
  - o Rachele Mussolini, Italian, wife of Benito Mussolini (b. 1890)
  - o "Orange Socks", unidentified murder victim (b. 1949-1964)
- October 31 – Edvin Adolphson, Swedish film actor/director (b. 1893)

November

Joyce Grenfell

- November 1
  - Bob Clayton, American television game show host & announcer (b. 1922)
  - Mamie Eisenhower, First Lady of the United States (b. 1896)
- November 2
  - Ernst Kals, German submarine commander (b. 1905)
  - Jacques Mesrine, French criminal; known as the "French Robin Hood" (b. 1936)
- November 3 – Hugh P. Harris, United States Army general (b. 1909)
- November 4
  - Morris Chalfen, American sports entertainment promoter (b. 1907)
  - Yank Terry, American baseball player (b. 1911)
- November 5 – Al Capp, American cartoonist (b. 1909)
- November 6 – Chick Evans, American golf champion (b. 1890)
- November 7 – Gyula Germanus, professor of oriental studies, a Hungarian writer and Islamologist of Jewish origin (b. 1884)
- November 8 – Yvonne de Gaulle, French political wife of former President of France Charles de Gaulle (b. 1900)
- November 9 – Louise Thaden, American aviator (b. 1905)
- November 9 – Tammy Jo Alexander, former unidentified murder victim (b. 1963)
- November 10 – Mahmud Al-Nashaf, Israeli-Arab politician (b. 1906)
- November 11 – Dimitri Tiomkin, Russian film composer (b. 1894)
- November 12 – Gavriil Veresov, Soviet chess player (b. 1912)
- November 13
  - Freda Betti, French opera singer (b.1924)
  - Ernest N. Harmon, American general (b. 1894)
- November 14
  - Amelia Best, Australian politician from Tasmania (b. 1900)
  - Grahame Budge, Canadian-born rugby player representing Scotland (b. 1920)
- November 15 – Ed Klieman, American baseball player; nicknamed, "Specs" (b. 1918)

- November 16 – Joseph Iglehart, American financier (b. 1891)
- November 17 – Immanuel Velikovsky, Russian author and psychiatrist (b. 1895)
- November 18
  - Freddie Fitzsimmons, American baseball player, manager, and coach (b. 1901)
  - Ade Schwammel, American football offensive tackle (b. 1908)
- November 19 – Dewey Jackson Short, Republican U. S. Representative from Missouri (b. 1898)
- November 21
  - Marie Byles, Australian conservationist (b. 1900)
  - Paul Wexler, American actor (b. 1929)
- November 22
  - Harry Jackman, Canadian politician and entrepreneur (b. 1900)
  - Irina Saburova, Russian poet, writer, and translator (b. 1907)
- November 23
  - Merle Oberon, British actress (b. 1911)
  - Judee Sill, American singer and cartoonist (b. 1944)
- November 24 – Georg Pinkepank, German Nazi Korvettenkapitän with the Kriegsmarine during World War II (b. 1907)
- November 25 – John S. Crawford, American politician for the Wisconsin State Assembly (b. 1923)
- November 26 – Marcel L'Herbier, French movie-maker (b. 1888)
- November 27 – Jerome Cavanagh, American civic politician; Mayor of Detroit, Michigan from (1962-1970), especially what doomed his administration was the July, 1967 race riots (b. 1928)
- November 28 – Peter Mulgrew, New Zealander mountaineer, yachtsman, and businessman (aircraft crash - Air New Zealand Flight 901 (b. 1927)
- November 29 – Zeppo Marx, American actor and comedian (b. 1901)
- November 30
  - Laura Gilpin, American photographer (b. 1891)
  - Joyce Grenfell, British actress and comedian (b. 1910)

- Gabrielle Dorziat, fashion trend setter in Paris and helped popularize the designs of Coco Chanel (b. 1880)

December

Richard Rodgers

Hafizullah Amin

- December 1
  - Noel Estrada, Puerto Rican composer (b. 1918)
  - Muhammad Abdel Moneim, Egyptian prince and former heir apparent (b. 1899)
- December 2 – Helen Fraser, Scottish born suffragist, feminist, educationalist (b. 1881)
- December 3 – Dhyan Chand, Indian hockey player (b. 1905)
- December 4
  - Dumitru Dan, Romanian geographer (b. 1889)

- ○ Petya Dubarova, Bulgarian poet (b. 1962)
- December 5
  - ○ Sonia Delaunay, Russian-French artist (b. 1885)
  - ○ Jesse Pearson, American actor (b. 1930)
- December 7 – Cecilia Payne-Gaposchkin, British-American astronomer and astrophysicist (b. 1900)
- December 8 – Nikolai Gritsenko, Soviet actor of Russian-Ukrainian background (b. 1912)
- December 9
  - ○ Freeman Harrison Owens, American cinematographer (b. 1890)
  - ○ Fulton J. Sheen, American Roman Catholic bishop (b. 1895)
- December 10 – Ann Dvorak, American actress (b. 1911)
- December 12 – Alan Shipman, English cricketer (b. 1901)
- December 13 – Jon Hall, American actor (b. 1915)
- December 14 – Ken Leishman, Canadian criminal (b. 1931)
- December 15 – Ethel Lackie, American Olympic swimmer (b. 1907)
- December 16 – Vagif Mustafazadeh, Azerbaijani jazz musician (b. 1940)
- December 17 – A. J. Iversen, Danish cabinetmaker (b. 1888)
- December 18
  - ○ Mohammad Mofatteh, Iranian philosopher (b. 1928)
  - ○ Franz Suchomel, Sudeten German Nazi Unterscharführer (b. 1907)
- December 19 – Donald Creighton, Canadian historian (b. 1902)
- December 21 – Ermindo Onega, Argentine footballer (b. 1940)
- December 22 – Darryl F. Zanuck, American film producer (b. 1902)
- December 23 – Peggy Guggenheim, American art collector (b. 1898)
- December 24 – Armand Massonet, Belgian painter (b. 1892)
- December 25
  - ○ Joan Blondell, American actress (b. 1906)
  - ○ Jordi Bonet, Canadian artist (b. 1932)
  - ○ Lee Bowman, American actor (b. 1914)

- December 26 – Karl Hubbuch, German painter, printmaker, and draftsman (b. 1891)
- December 27
  - Hafizullah Amin, General Secretary of the People's Democratic Party of Afghanistan, President of Afghanistan (b. 1929)
  - William H. Wilbur, United States Army officer (b. 1888)
- December 28 – Karl George (American football), American football player (b. 1894)
- December 29
  - Felix Becker, German Oberst for the Nazi's in World War II (b. 1893)
  - Richard Tecwyn Williams, Welsh biochemist (b. 1909)
- December 30 – Richard Rodgers, American composer (b. 1902)
- December 31 – John A. Powers, American public affairs officer for NASA (b. 1922)

Date unknown

- Dave Line, British author

Nobel Prizes

- Physics – Sheldon Lee Glashow, Abdus Salam, Steven Weinberg
- Chemistry – Herbert C. Brown, Georg Wittig
- Medicine – Allan M. Cormack, Godfrey N. Hounsfield
- Literature – Odysseas Elytis
- Peace – Mother Teresa
- Economics – Theodore Schultz, Arthur Lewis

In the News

USSR Invades Afghanistan.

Margaret Thatcher elected on May 3rd as the Prime minister in UK.

Michael Jackson releases his breakthrough album "Off the Wall" on August 10th.

Three Mile island Nuclear Accident after fire at reactor in Pennsylvania US.

63 Americans are taken hostage in the American Embassy in Tehran.

The Dictator Idi Amin is deposed in Uganda.

The Sahara Desert experiences snow for 30 minutes.

Pope John Paul II visits his native Poland, becoming the first Pope to visit a Communist country.

Lord Mountbatten and three others assassinated by the I.R.A.

Sony introduces the Sony Walkman costing $200.00.

The European Space Agency launches Ariane 1.

Sid Vicious, a former member of the Sex Pistols dies due to a heroin overdose during the trial for murdering his girlfriend.

Popular Films - Superman The Movie, Every Which Way But Loose, Rocky II, Alien, The Amityville Horror.

China institutes the one child per family rule to help control it's exploding population.

23 people die in Nice, France, when the coastal town is hit by a tsunami.

1979 Calendar

January 1979
Sun	Mon	Tue	Wed	Thu	Fri	Sat
	1	2	3	4	5	6
7	8	9	10	11	12	13
14	15	16	17	18	19	20
21	22	23	24	25	26	27
28	29	30	31			

February 1979
Sun	Mon	Tue	Wed	Thu	Fri	Sat
				1	2	3
4	5	6	7	8	9	10
11	12	13	14	15	16	17
18	19	20	21	22	23	24
25	26	27	28			

March 1979
Sun	Mon	Tue	Wed	Thu	Fri	Sat
				1	2	3
4	5	6	7	8	9	10
11	12	13	14	15	16	17
18	19	20	21	22	23	24
25	26	27	28	29	30	31

April 1979
Sun	Mon	Tue	Wed	Thu	Fri	Sat
1	2	3	4	5	6	7
8	9	10	11	12	13	14
15	16	17	18	19	20	21
22	23	24	25	26	27	28
29	30					

May 1979
Sun	Mon	Tue	Wed	Thu	Fri	Sat
		1	2	3	4	5
6	7	8	9	10	11	12
13	14	15	16	17	18	19
20	21	22	23	24	25	26
27	28	29	30	31		

June 1979
Sun	Mon	Tue	Wed	Thu	Fri	Sat
					1	2
3	4	5	6	7	8	9
10	11	12	13	14	15	16
17	18	19	20	21	22	23
24	25	26	27	28	29	30

July 1979
Sun	Mon	Tue	Wed	Thu	Fri	Sat
1	2	3	4	5	6	7
8	9	10	11	12	13	14
15	16	17	18	19	20	21
22	23	24	25	26	27	28
29	30	31				

August 1979
Sun	Mon	Tue	Wed	Thu	Fri	Sat
			1	2	3	4
5	6	7	8	9	10	11
12	13	14	15	16	17	18
19	20	21	22	23	24	25
26	27	28	29	30	31	

September 1979
Sun	Mon	Tue	Wed	Thu	Fri	Sat
						1
2	3	4	5	6	7	8
9	10	11	12	13	14	15
16	17	18	19	20	21	22
23	24	25	26	27	28	29
30						

October 1979
Sun	Mon	Tue	Wed	Thu	Fri	Sat
	1	2	3	4	5	6
7	8	9	10	11	12	13
14	15	16	17	18	19	20
21	22	23	24	25	26	27
28	29	30	31			

November 1979
Sun	Mon	Tue	Wed	Thu	Fri	Sat
				1	2	3
4	5	6	7	8	9	10
11	12	13	14	15	16	17
18	19	20	21	22	23	24
25	26	27	28	29	30	

December 1979
Sun	Mon	Tue	Wed	Thu	Fri	Sat
						1
2	3	4	5	6	7	8
9	10	11	12	13	14	15
16	17	18	19	20	21	22
23	24	25	26	27	28	29
30	31					

www.ingramcontent.com/pod-product-compliance
Lightning Source LLC
Chambersburg PA
CBHW060200290526
45789CB00003B/1099